Wanderings

Hilary Stringer

BookLeaf Publishing

Presentation by *BookLeaf Publishing*

Web: www.bookleafpub.com

E-mail: info@bookleafpub.com

ISBN: 978-93-95890-98-4

First edition 2022

DEDICATION

For my three wonderful daughters.

ACKNOWLEDGEMENT

To all those who have inspired me over the years.

PREFACE

Selecting twenty one poems from the many that I have written over the years has been an interesting amble down memory lane. Each one selected has a particular meaning for me. I am unlikely ever to get the call to be national poet laureate, but for me poetry has always been a way of distilling a moment, a feeling, a knowing into something more tangible. A small window into my thoughts at that time and place.

Roaches

Somewhere at the back of my mind
I have a memory of our future
A late spring afternoon
Lightest scent of columbine and campion
on the lightest breeze
Twenty paces before and behind the sound
Of laughter ricocheting from the trees
Rebounding echoes of stories drawn from
Private worlds, a filigree of silver dreams
Spun together on your flushed cheeks
And suntinged, agile limbs
As you explore the inside of your imagination

We walk down hidden paths and fox runs
Over dry stone bridges keeping toes
Tantalisingly away from the caress of coldest
Coldest, cleanest water in the stream
Watercress, waterlily, celandine
New names, crushed samples destined
For the old album at the back of the bookcase
Remembering the latin appellation
For this tiny white flower whispered by my
father
So I can pass on the knowledge
So you can pass on the knowledge
Timelines into the future

Climbing out of the meadow now
Catching beech nuts through the open toes
Of summer sandals I gave in and let you wear
Springing on the accumulated inches
Of melted leaves under the confident oak
Master of the hillside that creates its own shade
of brown
Not rust, not ochre, not bronze
A colour you can smell and touch
As we strike out for the pathway
Lovingly created by the forest ranger
To divert us from the quiet corner
Where the orchids share their rarest beauty

Rock outcrop at the half way point
A favourite since the time I was terrified
Of having only one pair of hands for a trio of
Precious, adventurous, fearless pirates
Giving peter pan and tinkerbell a run for their
money.
Older now and with the coordination
Of a feisty chamoix you race ahead
And conquer your own private Everest in granite
Leaving me breathless with admiration and
altitude
And a smile in my soul a mile wide
Collecting bilberries so that on return to base
camp

You can stain your lips with royal purple

Until we reach the turning to the right
That I always missed through looking down
Trying not to trip on jealous roots
That long to share the sunlight with the branches
Of the slender silver birch that line the way
But you are sure as ever and find the route
Tentative as you enter the green, moss covered
World of fissures and watercourses
Cold even in brilliant summer
Silent with the knowledge of centuries
Of subterfuge and escape from persecution
That hangs in the air as a reminder

Emerging again into the dappled light
Of perfect woodland, sounds and scents
Returning to the familiar and welcoming
We link arms and run without thought
Of how we look or if we'll fall
In each other's company is enough
To make the afternoon glow
And burn itself as a permanent record
Of how we four can be at ease in a place
In a time where we all know we'll never be
again
But that will last as iridescent shadows
And be there for your children

Firstborn

translucent hand
nails of perfect pearl
curled in the sleep
of the innocent

eyes tightly shut
still adjusting
to the harshness
of light
not mediated
by me

wrapped so tightly
by others
as I'm still scared
of breaking you

I had no idea
that this is what
love felt like

The power of two

The look on my face
Has entered the annals of legend
All those present will never forget
The shock of the revelation
Expecting one miracle
I was presented with two

So which came first?
Which of those tiny souls
First inhabited that space
And which was determined
Not to be left behind
Compelling strength of life

And as you grow
What will you become?
Your earliest days as boxers
Footballers, gymnasts
Choreographed movement
In such restricted circumstances

I yearn to meet you
One person made two
Or two become one?
Will the differences

Or the similarities
Be my greatest source of joy?

lifelong learning

making pancake rolls with one hand
finding new and exciting things to do
with pureed vegetables

carrying the weight of six telephone books on
one hip
waking when I've only had one hour's sleep in
24
to stop you crying

learning by heart the name, and gender, of
favourite toys
and spotting continuity errors in Disney films
perfectly proportioned french plaits
under wriggle pressure

hearing a new language as you master
consonants
making a jurassic fern from toilet roll and green
tissue
letting you whisk the cake mix when I know in
advance
that it will go all over the floor

crying real tears for the woman in the news
who's lost a child
wanting to land on Mayfair with two hotels
explaining god, sex and death in one
conversation
in words of less than three syllables

finding out that love expands to fill the space
available
what will you teach me tomorrow?

A first Barbie doll

Unexpected
She's only three
A gift from her petite amie
Unwelcome
Just not pc
Pink, deformed, a travesty

Confusion
Feminist mood
Solidarity with the sisterhood
Consider
if removal would
devastate my precious brood

Truimphant
In her cherub's eyes
Delight of owning special prize
Protective
Lest I might chastise
Action Man - demilitarised

Defeated
Mother stops and sees
That plastic girl with bendy knees
Conquering

Barefaced duplicity
Comes with spare accessories…..

The cupboard raiders

Call the police, go dial 999
They're both under age, they'll get off with a fine
Caught right in the act, their hand in the till
Well, hands in the cupboard, same principle still
Called out for a second, walked into the hall
Kids playing contented, no signals at all
That on my return I'd find both on the steal...
"Dinner too late? Mother failed with the meal?
Well we're only one but we're hungry as hell
She left, turned her back, and she taught us so well
That food's on the shelves, comes in bright coloured packets
And if we're quite careful we won't make a racket"
But no! Much too slow. Caught forever, freeze frame
My two little angels, turned devils! The shame!

Rhyming

There's something I should tell you
I'd like you to know
To make you smile
(and what a smile)
That when we
Talk
Listen
Laugh
Share
You are my mirror
I can see in my reflection
That I will find balance again
And I'm not sure I understand why
But you've made my poems rhyme

Starting over

It's hard after fifteen years of not being
to learn how to be with others
Compulsory re-education programme
in basic social skills
Lesson one in eye contact
Chapter three on saying yes
Advanced courses in self-esteem to chase out
denial that you might find me pleasant company
…..and laugh at my jokes
Crash course in staying awake past nine o'clock
when Horlicks and slippers call

Ghosts

They inhabit the white space between
the blue notes, where cadences of half
remembered melodies and fragments
of familiar verses compete for attention.
As the picture takes form in my memory
Of the first place and time I heard these words,
These climbing chords, so images of you
Come back to complete the replay.
And what was it that you used to sing
In defiance of the lyrics on the sleeve?
A shaping of the words to make me smile
Interplay of the written with the known
Weaving its own special magic now
As the artist sings your version, not his own
And as the song unfolds I feel the touch
Of you as once it came so light so soft
Around my shoulders as we danced
For no one else except ourselves

Clouds

Vapour trails intertwined
as the residue of passage
of hopeful journeys
dissipates in the rarified air
Light sparkling from the crystal haze
that spreads ever more thinly
to the edges of perception
Sea of possibilities
Shapes glimpsed as they
form and reform on
the soaring columns of air
Caught in the iridescent sunlight
perfect droplets drawn
to each other for fear of falling
and buoyed by the warmth
of the tilled ground below
Shifting and roiling as if
afraid to reveal their true form
the layers shear and part
to create a landscape of
fantasy and imagination
its identity in the beholder's sight
Unique and transitory
carried on the winds and
defined by the currents

A wilderness of spun sugar
raw cotton and silk
stretches ahead to follow
the curvature of the earth
At once uniform and infinitely varied
a carpet of welcoming softness
over which we fly in awe
and where angels tread
as we gaze to the distant horizon

Seascape

Existential tension
between the solid and the liquid
Constant motion of water
Worrying at the tight packed grains
Until they form into a frown of ridges and rills
To capture the unwary foam
As it tries to retreat into the safety
Of the collective depths of the sea.

Unmerciful movement
That polishes hard granite
Consumes softer targets through
Gentle lapping, more deadly
Than turbulent storm-whipped rage
Leaving perfect smoothness
Modest jewels of the margins
Sparkling when wet

Jealous collector
Of all things transitory
The acquisitive tendencies
Of a bower bird, hoarding
In lines that mark your territory
The bounty of the discarded
Broken and forgotten treasures

Long distance travellers

Secret gardener
Of a multitude of shapes and forms
Delicate fingers of seagrass
Swaying in the watery breeze
Black and brittle once parted
From the nurturing brine
Shredding the feet of the unwary
Who try to get too close

Perfect smoothness
On a still, summer day
Luring distant watchers to try
Their luck in the crystal shallows
Breathless withdrawal to the mellow sand
As the bite of atlantic reminds us
That like the iceberg you show
Only a fraction of yourself

Feather pillow

Luxurious softness
Yielding to my touch
As I pour myself
Into your soft embrace
Holding me close while
I journey into the unknown
Dreamscape of sleep
A form of your own
Selflessly subjugated
To others' needs
Taking on the shape
And character
Of your possessor
How you must long
For morning when
You can be yourself again
Or do you thrive
On giving pleasure?

the benefits of wine

I think sometimes that in my rhymes
I'll find the key to liking me
I'll find a way through what I say
Towards a sense of consequence
To leave behind work of some kind
That makes me feel that I was real
A person who (apart from you)
The world might say had a part to play
And then perchance it might enhance
My self belief.... A huge relief
But then I think I'll have a drink
And swap analysis for a spot of paralysis

Vehicular incompatibility

I've read all the books
From Venus to Mars
I've come to believe
That we're more like cars

You're a Mercedes
I'm a 2CV
You're all electric
I'm utility

You're packed with gadgets
I'm bolt together
You're climate controlled
I let in the weather

I saunter along
While you race away
I make people smile
While you make them pay

Important to find
A road for us two
Before the 12,000 mile
Service is due

paradox

For any normal solid body
The laws of physics state
That its impact on surroundings is
In proportion to its weight
But ask any woman on the street
How well those laws apply
To those whose figure although fine
Does not in size comply
With some ideal in magazines
And in the minds of men
Of bosom full and bottom tight
And less than a size ten
For if you dare to buck the trend
To call the image risible
You run the risk of fading out
Of being quite invisible
For no-one sees beyond the shell
The person that's the same
As once she was when she was slim
Her size a source of shame
So they ignore you, pass you by
No glances 'cross the bar
No heads that turn nor whistles loud
Blank space is all you are

Getting to the bottom of it

They say that travel
Broadens the mind.
In my experience
From extensive field testing
On long-haul flights
Under swaying palms
In tapas bars
Outside Greek tavernas
A la carte
And antipasti
That travel
Also broadens your hips

In reply to Delia Smith

What I want to know is
Why your souffles always rise
How the fruit in your fruitcake
Never sinks to the bottom
If your sauces are really perfect
every time
When every real woman that I know
Has charcoal on the oven shelves
Burns on her wrists
And spatters on page 26
'easy pancake batter'

Roma woman

Darkness of your skin
Reflects a deep space in your soul
Forced into a life unnatural
You exist in this cityscape
A stranger to captivity
Wild soul yearning for release
Compelled by the hand of others.
The child you carry
A curiosity, a miracle
Astounding in her beauty
Fair of hair and dark complexion
Time spent in the unforgiving sun
A draw so strong I could not resist
I let the connection be made
The golden filament that binds us all
Let both of you inside to see
My longing, indecision, anguish
And you gave me my release
Would that I could have given you yours

Facades

City of all times, made and unmade by changing
days
Under your unyielding streets the secrets of
another age
For you grow, adapt, take from what once was
what you need for tomorrow
Wherein lies your essence? What defines the
meaning of you?
From the outside, baroque magnificence,
classical proportion
Homage to one god and the older gods who
formed your destiny
Cold marble, frozen statues, grandeur meant to
keep at bay
The ambitions of the inconsequential
But behind the facades what do you reveal if I
look beyond
The well-trod thoroughfares?
Tangles of vein-like back streets, intersecting,
meandering
Joining in wide lacunae to rest, talk, revive, in
the blistering heat
Life blood of the city carried through barely
visible passageways
Faded paint, shades of the setting sun

Broken shutters, rampant vines
A city lived in by those who love
Who have loved through the ages
Whose duty maintains the outward view of a proud world city
Whose passion allows nature to take its course

Lost and found

In a far away place
In a time that will not come again
I searched for myself
In distant places
Remote places
Dark forests, high mountains
Wave torn coastlines
But also in cities
Where the people were as many
As the days and nights I dreamed
And though I saw many things
And many of those were in me
I did not find myself

So I searched for myself in intimacy
In giving of myself
Within tight boundaries
Amphora of bounties
Unquenchable fount
I poured from myself all that was good
Fresh, tender, nurturing
And for a time it grew
Sustained on the strength
Of all that I released
Roots of that growth in turn

Passing back into my vital nature
But ere long, those very roots
Began to envelop and overwhelm
Pot-bound and hungry
And so I closed the source
All life ceased for them
And also for me

Denuded of the outer shell
Mantle of conformity
That shows we belong
I wandered for a time undone
Lightness of being returning
Steps an inch above the ground
Half way between expectations
Too hard to sustain, I reached for another
Beautiful mirage of promises
Mirror of my potential
Where all I valued
Was valued also
And for a time
In dreams and waking
I saw a glimpse of me

Fractured now
Laying in fragments all around me
The way starts to become clear
From those high mountains
Endless giving

Reflected light
The construct of my being starts to coalesce
The need to search
In times that will never come again
Retreats
Here is where I must look again

Alone

Sometimes, when darkness falls
I hear the silence drawing in
Feeling of smooth velvet
Smelling of incense
In that stillness
A part of me is released
From physical bounds
My quiet self reaches out
Tendrils of thought
Gentle
Confident of finding you
I am alone in this place
I wait for the picture to form
A shadow of faraway feelings
For I know that you are holding me
In a distant bed

www.ingramcontent.com/pod-product-compliance
Lightning Source LLC
Chambersburg PA
CBHW051749130826
49812CB00033B/1067
* 9 7 8 9 3 9 5 8 9 0 9 8 4 *